Tag! Get Me!

by Verne Greene
illustrated by Cam Mai

Practice Decodable 27

McGraw Hill Education

Bothell, WA • Chicago, IL • Columbus, OH • New York, NY

MHEonline.com

Send all inquiries to:
McGraw-Hill Education
8787 Orion Place
Columbus, OH 43240

ISBN: 978-0-02-145779-3
MHID: 0-02-145779-4

Printed in the United States of America.

7 8 9 CTM 23

Fun Games

We like fun games.
We like tag.

We have lots of kids.
We go and hide.

Can you see five kids?
We have lots of fun!

Tag!

What do I like best?

I like to hide!

Brave Liv likes to be "it."

Can Liv even see me yet?

Best Game

Liv dives at me.

Tag! Liv got me!

What game do you like best?